Steam in
SOMERSET

Derek Huntriss

First published 1996

ISBN 0711 0 2479 0

© Derek Huntriss 1996

Published by Ian Allan Publishing

An imprint of Ian Allan Ltd,
Terminal House, Station Approach, Shepperton, Surrey TW17 8AS;
and printed by Ian Allan Printing Ltd., Coombelands House,
Coombelands Lane, Addlestone, Surrey KT15 1HY.

IAN ALLAN
Publishing

Front Cover:
On a clear summer's day former S&D Class '7F' 2-8-0
No 53807 heads northeast for Bath (Green Park) with
the 10.40am (SO) from Exmouth to Cleethorpes past
Wellow on 25 August 1962.   *Roy Hobbs*

Rear Cover:
4-6-0 No 1028 *County of Warwick* leaves Castle Cary
station with an up freight on 17 September 1962. In the
consist is 0-6-0PT No 9497 on its last journey to
Swindon before cutting up.   *Alan Jarvis*

This Page:
On the Somerset side of Whiteball tunnel 4-6-0 No 4978
Westwood Hall heads the 9.40am from Birmingham
(Snow Hill) to Paignton on 9 September 1962.
                                    Peter W. Gray

Introduction

Today the County of Somerset is better known for its cricket, cheese and cider. Back in the 1600s the talk in the northern part of the region was not of willow and leather, but the extraction of coal. The real expansion of the mining industry was signalled by the opening of Old Pit at Radstock in 1763 and although that pit closed in 1854 the coalfield at its peak went on to produce 1,750,000 tons annually.

It was the businessmen of Bristol who were amongst the most important promoters of the Great Western and Bristol & Exeter railways whose lines were to criss-cross the county in addition to those of the London & South Western Railway. Then there was the cross-country link from Bath to Bournemouth established by the now legendary Somerset & Dorset Joint Railway. Born in 1862 the Somerset & Dorset Railway was an amalgamation between the Somerset Central Railway and the Dorset Central Railway. It was anticipated that substantial traffic would be attracted to this link between the English Channel and the Bristol Channel. When this traffic did not materialise it gambled everything on the building of its extension from Evercreech Junction to Bath to join up with the Midland Railway. It was this expense that brought about the end of S&D's independence and in 1875 it was leased to the Midland Railway and L&SWR as equal partners in a Joint Committee.

At the Grouping in 1923 the leasing arrangement came to an end and the Joint Committee became legally owned by the successors of the MR and L&SWR — the LMS and Southern Railways — and eventually became part of British Railways upon Nationalisation.

This title aims to offer a colour portrait of BR lines in Somerset as they were operated under steam between 1957 and 1966 together with pictures of industrial locomotives that were still in use after that date. The first part takes the reader on a journey over the Somerset & Dorset line from Bath (Green Park) to Henstridge, after which the line passed into Dorset, the second taking a general look at the many lines that criss-crossed the county on both the Western and Southern Regions of BR.

Of all the railways that once existed in Somerset, only the basic framework has now passed into the new era of privatisation, the eventual outcome of these political changes will only be judged by future generations. However, the efforts of preservationists at three sites in the county — The Somerset & Dorset Museum Trust, The West Somerset Railway and the East Somerset Railway — keep the memories of the working steam railway alive.

Bibliography

R. H. Clark: *An Historical Survey of Selected Great Western Stations Layouts and Illustrations Volumes 1 to 3;* OPC

C. J. Gammell: *Great Western Branch Lines 1955-1965;* OPC

Mac Hawkins: *The Somerset & Dorset Then and Now ;* Guild Publishing

Industrial Railway Society: *Industrial Locomotives of South Western England*

C. W. Judge and C. R. Potts: *An Historical Survey of the Somerset & Dorset Railway Track Layouts and Illustrations;* OPC

E. Lyons: *An Historical Survey of Great Western Engine Sheds 1947;* OPC

Colin G. Maggs: *The Last Years of the Somerset & Dorset;* Ian Allan

Ivo Peters: *The Somerset & Dorset An English Cross Country Railway:*

Ivo Peters: *The Somerset & Dorset in the Fifties 1950-1954 — Volume 1*

Ivo Peters: *The Somerset & Dorset in the Fifties 1955-1959 — Volume 2*

Ivo Peters: *The Somerset & Dorset in the Sixties 1960-1962 — Volume 3*

Ivo Peters: *The Somerset & Dorset in the Sixties 1963-1966 — Volume 4*

All Ivo Peters titles published by OPC

C. R. Potts: *An Historical Survey of Selected Great Western Stations Layouts and Illustrations;* OPC

R. C. Riley: *The Colour of Steam Volume 2 The Somerset & Dorset Line;* Atlantic Transport Publishers

Martin Smith: *The Railways of Bristol & Somerset;* Ian Allan

Acknowledgements

The author offers his sincere thanks to the many dedicated photographers whose work appears in these pages, in particular to Dick Riley without whose contribution, the title would not have been possible.

In addition to these photographers, I must also offer my thanks to fellow enthusiast and former Coventrian, Graham Hooper, for the loan of numerous text books on the subject, without which the captions could not have been written.

Sincere thanks also go to Colin Maggs, well respected author on this subject, for sharing his in-depth knowledge.

Derek Huntriss
Camborne
Cornwall
June 1996

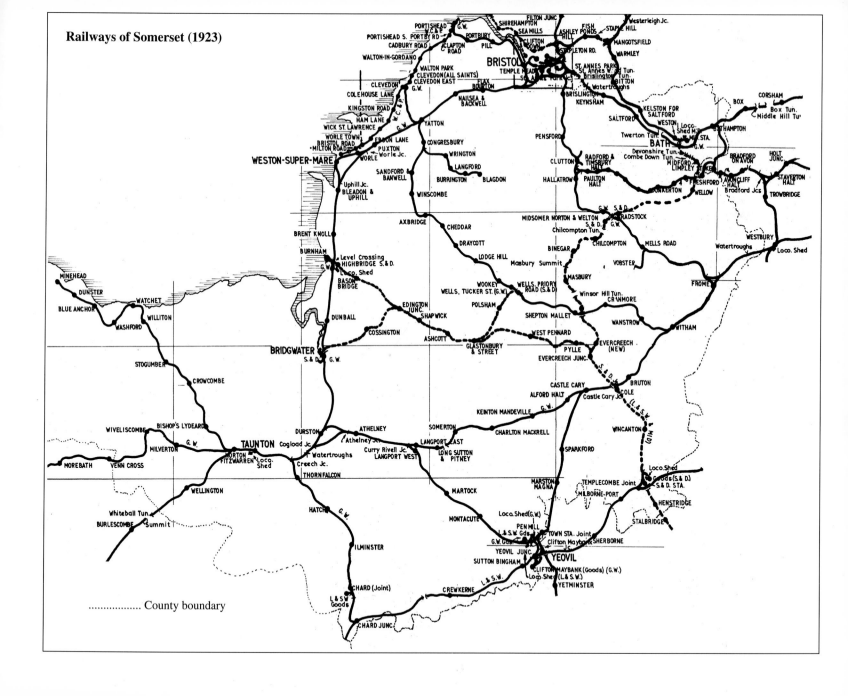

Railways of Somerset (1923)

.... County boundary

Left: The Georgian-style exterior of Bath (Green Park) station taken on 5 July 1959. Built from Bath stone, the station was opened on 3 August 1869 and at that time the terminus was at the end of the 10-mile long branch of the Midland Railway from Mangotsfield. The station was shared with the extension of the S&D from Evercreech Junction from 20 July 1874. A four-road station under an arched glass roof which extended to about half the length of the platform. Having only two platform faces, the two centre roads were used for running round and stabling. After closure in 1966 the station fell into dereliction and decay despite its status as a Grade 2 Listed building. Eventually sold by BR to Bath City Council in late 1979, the latter reached an agreement with J. Sainsbury plc who at enormous cost carried out a superb restoration.   *R. C. Riley*

Above: BR Standard Class '3' 2-6-2T No 82038 prepares to depart from Bath (Green Park) with the 12.25pm train to Bristol on a very damp 2 November 1963. Today the train shed operates as a car park for shoppers at Sainsbury's supermarket and after some £1,500,000 and 44 weeks was spent on restoration, Green Park was formally re-opened by HRH Princess Margaret on 1 December 1982.   *Bill Potter*

Above: The last survivor, Class '1P' 0-4-4T No 58086 is seen in store at Bath in September 1960. In the early 1950s Johnson 0-4-4Ts were still used for handling most Highbridge branch passenger trains. Of four class members allocated to Highbridge, all had been reboilered with the exception of No 58047 which retained its round topped firebox and Salter valves. *R.E. Toop*

Right: S&D '7F' 2-8-0 No 53804 has been specially prepared to work a Stephenson Locomotive Society special and is depicted outside Bath MPD on Sunday 11 September 1960. Scheduled to run from Bath down to Templecombe, No 53804 had to run 'wrong-line' from Chilcompton to Binegar because of engineering work. At Chilcompton the special had to set back to the up road while the points were being clipped, the pilotman regaining the footplate after this exercise had been carried out. From the beginning of the 1960s the popularity of running enthusiast specials over the Somerset & Dorset had increased, the organisers often requesting that motive power should be a former S&D Class '7F' 2-8-0. *Alan Jarvis*

BR Standard Class '9F' 2-10-0 No 92220 is seen outside Bath MPD on 8 September 1962 as it is being prepared to work the last down 'Pines Express'. From contemporary reports the departure from Green Park was described as explosive, the crew having already been dissuaded from collecting an empty coach to add to what was already a full load. The departure could be described as being explosive in two senses, firstly the quantity of detonators that were exploded and the most enthusiastic driving. During the stop at Evercreech Junction someone had hung a pine wreath on the locomotive's smokebox door.   *Bill Potter*

Every winter one of Bath MPD's allocation of 'Jinty' 0-6-0 tanks would be prepared to act as 'snow-plough engine' should the S&D have a snowfall deep enough to necessitate its use. A regular candidate for this duty was No 47557, depicted here inside Bath shed on 8 February 1959. This loco had been taken off shunting duties as its preparation required the removal of its buffers front and rear before the ploughs were fitted.

At this time the Somerset & Dorset had come under the control of the Western Region, ex-GWR types being introduced with differing degrees of success. These measures were meant to replace the ageing S&D 2-8-0s. An initial trial with an ex-WD 'Austerity' 2-8-0 ended when the locomotive's brakes proved inadequate. The engine selected for this test was No 90125 and was despatched with the 11am Bath to

Evercreech Junction goods on 22 January 1959. Six vacuum fitted vans had been included next to the engine. These were brought into action after passing Priestleigh at speed when the locomotive's brakes no longer had control of the train. A similar fate was to befall an ex-GWR 0-6-2T, the only success of ex-GWR locomotives was the ability of 0-6-0PTs to take over the shunting of Bath goods yard.   *Trevor B. Owen*

Above: BR Standard Class '4' 4-6-0 No 75023 pilots 'West Country' Pacific No 34042 *Dorchester* with a Bradford to Bournemouth train up the 1 in 50 to Devonshire tunnel on 8 September 1962. The introduction of Bulleid Light Pacifics on to the S&D had begun in 1951 when No 34109 *Sir Trafford Leigh-Mallory* had been used for trials in March of that year.

At that time No 34109 was less than one year old having entered service in May 1950. With the Southern Region being responsible for motive power on the S&D, four Bulleid Light Pacifics were allocated to Bath MPD following these trials. Up until that time all locomotives on the S&D had been on loan from the London Midland Region.   *Bill Potter*

Right: The 'Pines Express' is seen leaving Combe Down tunnel on 25 August 1962 behind BR Standard Class '4' 4-6-0 No 75023 and an unidentified Unrebuilt Bulleid Light Pacific. Like Devonshire tunnel, the bore in Combe Down tunnel was very restricted and had no ventilation shafts. The longest tunnel on the line, Combe Down ran for just over one mile. *Alan Jarvis*

Left: BR Standard Class '4' 2-6-0 No 76026 heads the 1.8pm (SO) Bournemouth to Bristol across Midford viaduct on 25 August 1962. Whilst no engine of this class was ever allocated to a depot on the S&D, they had worked regularly over the line since 1955. Situated just south of the station, the eight-arch Midford viaduct carried the S&D over the Somersetshire Coal Canal, and the Limpley Stoke to Camerton branch which featured in the film 'The Titfield Thunderbolt'.   *A.Jarvis*

Above: A classic view of the S&D at Midford as BR Standard Class '9F' 2-10-0 No 92245 heads the 7.43am (SO) Bradford to Bournemouth on 25 August 1962.The single line section from Bath Junction came to an end at Midford, although the station was still on the single line. As can be seen in this picture the double track started towards the south end of the viaduct. From Midford the S&D remained double track for the next 32 miles to Templecombe running southwest towards

Radstock through the Midford and Wellow valleys. Over this section the gradient was constantly undulating, one reverse curve following another in quick succession as the line followed the contours of the hillsides. Much of this undulating course was because it was built on the towpath of a former branch of the Somerset Coal Canal. The tramway was used for conveying coal mined around Radstock to the canal at Midford.   *Alan Jarvis*

Above: The late Percy Savage, a kind and dedicated railwayman, prepares the tablet catching apparatus at Midford for action. This mechanism was patented by Alfred Whitaker in 1905 during his period as Locomotive Superintendent of the Joint Line from 1889 to 1911. The 16 lever signalbox was built well into the hillside at an extremely attractive location. It was unusual in that it had a flat roof which was the result of its partial demolition by an errant Class '3F' 0-6-0 No 7620 which ran away with eight wagons on 29 July 1936. The crew of this locomotive had failed to close the regulator and had leapt from their engine in an effort to protect themselves from a collision which seemed inevitable but did not actually take place at Writhlington Colliery Sidings near Radstock. The box was always kept immaculate until closure. *R. C. Riley*

Right: BR Standard Class '4' 4-6-0 No 75027 pilots an unidentified Rebuilt Bulleid Light Pacific with a down express through the curves south of Midford station on 25 August 1962. No 75027 differed from the Standard Class 4s allocated to Bath MPD in that it was painted green and was fitted with one of the smaller tenders. Happily No 75027 survived into the preservation era and now is based on the Bluebell Railway. *Alan Jarvis*

Left: One of three BR Standard Class '4s' allocated to Bath MPD in 1956, No 75072, in double chimney form, nears Midford with the 3.40pm Bournemouth West to Bristol on 12 August 1961. The double blast-pipe and chimney had been fitted at Eastleigh Works during a General Repair in December 1960. Both No 75073 and No 75072 remained in traffic at Bath MPD until withdrawn in December 1965 after which they were placed in store at Templecombe. *R. C. Riley*

Above: Having cleared the single line section at Midford, Class '4F' 0-6-0 No 44523 continues to assist former SDJR Class '7F' 2-8-0 No 53801 with the 9.8am Birmingham to Bournemouth West on 5 September 1959. At that time Class '2P' 4-4-0s were the regular pilot locomotives, the Class '4F' 0-6-0s being pressed into traffic when the regular motive power was in short supply. Up until 1952 the S&D Class '7F' 2-8-0s had only been used on passenger

work when there was no alternative. These matters changed with the arrival of Mr. Webb the new shedmaster at Bath MPD. During 1952 he made wide use of the '7Fs' for passenger work, both as train engine and as pilots. From this time onwards the '7Fs' were allowed to take 10 coaches unassisted over the Mendips. Having left the single line section, the pair allowed Class '2P' No 40700 and BR Standard Class '5' No 73051 to proceed north. *R. C. Riley*

Below: The crew of S&D Class '7F' 2-8-0 No 53807 take a well-earned break after setting back their freight into the up sidings at Wellow as BR Standard Class '5' No 73049 passes with the up 'Pines Express' on 6 July 1959. The class of 2-8-0s had been built in two batches, S&DJR Nos 80-85 (BR Nos 53800-5) were built at Derby in 1914 and the larger boilered Nos 86-90 (BR Nos 53806-10) were built by Robert Stephenson & Co. of Darlington in 1925. By autumn 1955 all of the 1925 series had been fitted with the smaller boiler.

Right: No 53807 restarts its freight for Bath from Wellow. Some 6 ¾ miles from Bath (Green Park), the station at Wellow was always well used as buses only served the village once a week.

Both: R.C. Riley

Left: A superb portrait of Radstock North taken on 12 July 1960. Opened on 20 July 1874, the S&D station at Radstock North never had any physical connection to its adjacent GWR neighbour until the closure of the S&D in 1966, when a connection was built for the coal traffic from Writhlington Colliery to Portishead. The layout at Radstock North was quite extensive and was controlled by two signalboxes,

originally known as Radstock East and Radstock West although renamed Radstock North 'A' and North 'B' respectively in 1951. The level crossing seen in this picture was controlled by North 'B' signal box and was close to a similar level crossing at the adjacent GWR station, the pair being responsible for miles of traffic jams in the summer months. Radstock North remained open for passengers until 7 March 1966.

Above: LMS 'Jinty' No 47557 is depicted again, this time on 26 September 1959 where it is seen from the brake van at Radstock North as it prepares to bank on the climb to Masbury summit. At Binegar the banker picked up a wrong line staff for its return working light. Just before Masbury summit the Goods Guard would uncouple the banker with the aid of the hook visible on No 47557's smokebox door. *Both: R.C. Riley*

Above: One of two very low bodied Sentinels ordered by the LMS in 1929, No 47190, is seen at Radstock on 22 July 1958. The need for these locomotives arose from having to pass under the extremely low arch of Tyning Bridge, known locally to S&D men as 'Marble Arch'. This bridge had the very restricted clearance of 10ft 10in from rail level to the roof of the arch which prevented the 'Jinty' 0-6-0s from reaching the colliery sidings beyond. The unorthodox design of the four whee, geared chain-drive Sentinel included the positioning of its vertical boiler in the cab, a feature which was unbearable to work in except for the months in the depth of winter. These shunters had replaced Radstock's ageing shunters of 1885/1895 and were themselves withdrawn in 1959 and 1961 by which time the arch had been demolished.

Right: S&D '7F' 2-8-0 No 53810 is engaged in its normal duty of hauling goods traffic at Midsomer Norton South on 3 July 1961. Here it will stop for Class '3F' 0-6-0 No 47316 to add its load of coal wagons from Norton Hill Colliery. Midsomer Norton was best known for its appearance, in particular the station gardens, winning first prize for the 'Best Kept Station' year after year. *Both: R. C. Riley*

Class '2P' No 40564 pilots BR Standard Class '5' No 73052 as they approach Chilcompton tunnel with the 8.50am Bradford to Bournemouth West on 1 July 1961. At this time there was an abundance of carriage stock on BR available for Saturday workings, several of the through trains over the S&D would be used for a single journey, remaining in sidings at either destination point until the following Saturday.

The southbound climb had eased briefly to 1 in 300 through Midsomer Norton after which the gradient steepened again to 1 in 53 up to Chilcompton tunnel as the S&D continued to climb higher and higher into the Mendips. Where possible the line followed the lie of the land but ¾ mile south of Chilcompton a short tunnel was necessary to pass under a bluff in the hillside. Chilcompton tunnel, 66yd long, was originally built as a single bore but was later doubled, the up and down roads being separate.

After the tunnel the climb steepened even further to 1 in 50 culminating in a very difficult stretch where the line curved upwards through a rock cutting before reaching Chilcompton station. Once again easing to 1 in 300 through Chilcompton station, it immediately reverted to 1 in 50 beyond the platform.

R. C. Riley

A delightful portrait of the well-kept signal box at Chilcompton taken on 1 September 1962. An unusual feature of the box was the absence of shunting signals, these movements being carried out by hand signals. At Chilcompton station there was a goods shed adjacent to the goods yard and a large water tower used by banking engines returning to Radstock. An additional siding on the down side gave access for coal brought by road from New Rock colliery and loaded on to rail wagons. The station at Chilcompton closed to passengers on 7 March 1966, the 13-lever box closing on 11 April 1965.

Alan Jarvis

Below: With the date for closure set for 7 March 1966 the Locomotive Club of Great Britain organised a farewell special for the last Saturday of operations, 5 March. Here Unrebuilt Bulleid Light Pacifics Nos 34006 *Bude* and 34057 *Biggin Hill* approach Winsor Hill tunnel with the special. It had arrived at Templecombe after running down the Southern main line, the immaculate Pacifics being used for the trip up to Evercreech Junction where two Ivatt 2-6-2Ts took over for the return trip to Highbridge. On return to Evercreech Junction the Pacifics took charge again for the run up to Bath and in the late afternoon set off south from Bath for the final run over the S&D. From 7 March 1966 much of the Somerset & Dorset line running 71½ miles from Bath to Bournemouth over the Mendip Hills closed to traffic for ever.

Right: Also on 5 March 1966 Ivatt Class '2' 2-6-2T No 41307 and BR Standard Class '4' 2-6-4T No 80138 approach Winsor Hill tunnel with the 2pm from Templecombe to Bath. With the imminent closure only one day away, as many engines as possible were being worked back to Bath MPD. All trains on this day were packed out with people enjoying their last ride over the line. *Both: Roy Hobbs*

Ex-S&DJR Class '7F' 2-8-0 No 53805 takes water at Shepton Mallet at the southern end of the down platform as it heads the 12.35pm freight from Bath on 26 September 1959. On the northern approach to Shepton Mallet was the 118yd long Bath Road viaduct, one side of which collapsed during a gale in February 1946. The rebuilding of this viaduct was not completed until the August of that year, the intervening period seeing the use of single line working from the temporary Waterloo Road signalbox. This was a reminder that the line was once wholly single, the up side viaduct remaining intact. Just south of Charlton Road station the S&D passed under the GWR's line which connected Witham, on the Westbury to Taunton section of the main line to Devon and Cornwall, with Yatton on the Bristol to Taunton main line. The 26-lever signalbox at Shepton Mallet stood on the down side next to a small waiting room. The station closed to goods traffic on 10 June 1963. *R. C. Riley*

For the summer holiday traffic between 1960 and 1962 the WR allocated four BR Standard Class '9F' 2-10-0s to work between Bath and Evercreech Junction unassisted with trains up to 410 tons. Here the porter at Evercreech New watches as No 92001 heads the 10.32am Bournemouth West to Manchester on 28 July 1962. Outside of the summer services the '9Fs' were not retained as they were not fitted for steam heating trains. The tall attractive signalbox situated stood on the up platform. This box, having 26 levers, was the second box at this station and was closed from 7 March 1966.   *R. C. Riley*

Left: Bulleid 'West Country' class Pacific No 34044 *Woolacombe* stands at the head of an up empty stock working at Evercreech Junction on 6 July 1959. First allocated to the line in 1951, the suitability of the Bulleid Light Pacifics for the line was soon in doubt when their tendency to slip became apparent. Although they ceased to be allocated to Bath, they continued to work on the line from the Bournemouth end.

R. C. Riley

Above: One of two members of the class to survive into preservation, S&D 2-8-0 No 53809 takes water at Evercreech Junction on 1 September 1962. At this date No 53809 was one of only five members of the class to survive. No 53809 was saved from the scrapyard by Mr Frank Beaumont and has been expertly restored to running order and can be seen in operation at the head-quarters of the Midland Railway Trust at Butterley near Derby. Trains entering Evercreech Junction from Bath

had to slow to 25mph as they took the sharp left hand curve whereas those from the single line branch from Highbridge had a straight approach, this reflecting the original main line status of the branch. The '7F' 2-8-0s were frequently rostered to work freight trains up to Westerleigh Yard, north of Mangotsfield, on the Bristol to Gloucester line.

Alan Jarvis

Above: The 4.15pm Templecombe to Bath formed of SR Maunsell coaching stock approaches Evercreech Junction behind Crewe-built Class '4F' 0-6-0 No 44135 on 6 July 1959. This picture was taken from the tall South signalbox which having 26 levers controlled a level crossing and access to the goods yard.
R .C. Riley

Right: BR Class '9F' 2-10-0 No 92233 passes the stone supported water tank at Evercreech Junction as it heads the 7.35am (SO) Nottingham to Bournemouth (West) on 1 September 1962. A similar water tank at Shepton Mallet bore a cast-iron plate with the surprising inscription 'S&D 1892 WIMBLEDON IRON WORKS'. The footbridge visible in this picture connected the two platforms, the down platform having the attractive stone built station buildings and the large stationmaster's house. The station and buildings were put up for sale by tender by BR in 1970 and a reply to the newspaper advertisement offering a mere £5,050 secured them. Today neatly placed bushes adorn the platforms and trackbed.
Alan Jarvis

After the Johnson Class '1P' 0-4-4Ts had disappeared from the S&D scene, the working of the Templecombe to Highbridge passenger services was put into the hands of Ivatt 2-6-2Ts and Johnson '3F' 0-6-0s. Here Ivatt Class '2MT' No 41248 passes over Cole viaduct with the 1.15 up local to Highbridge from Templecombe on 18 July 1959. As the WR increased its influence on the branch services, ex-GWR Collett 0-6-0s were transferred to replace the '3F' 0-6-0s. Cole is of considerable historical railway interest in that it was the most northerly station on the former Dorset Central Railway. In 1862 this company amalgamated with the Somerset Central Railway, which ran from just north of Cole to Burnham, to form the Somerset & Dorset Railway. The main building at Cole was located on the down platform and was of typical Dorset Central design being built of stone with high gables and tall chimneys.

R. C. Riley

Collett 0-6-0 No 2277 leaves Cole with the 2.20pm from Highbridge to Templecombe on 1 September 1962. These 0-6-0s were drafted to the line as WR branches closed or became dieselised, often surviving for just a few months before withdrawal. Whilst much of their work was typically that of the Class `3Fs', the drivers preferred the Ivatt 2-6-2Ts which remained until closure. It can also be seen that the coaches are of GWR origin.

R.C. Riley

Left: LMS Class '4F' 0-6-0 No 44422 arrives at Cole in superb evening light with the 4.37pm from Bath to Templecombe on 18 July 1959. Another feature of S&D individuality was the headlamp code for passenger trains being the same for both local and express. The small 14-lever wooden signalbox at Cole, built in LSWR style, was situated at the southern end of the up platform. Being equipped with a block switch, it controlled the small goods yard on the down side and also broke the section from Evercreech Junction South to Wincanton. On the up platform was a small wooden shelter which stood on an extension at a slightly higher level of the former short up platform. The yard at Cole closed on 5 April 1965, the signal box being closed on 31 May 1965.

Above: The delightful flower bed and ornamental pond at Cole, the pride of station staff, photographed on 28 July 1962. Having remained empty for many years after closure, the station building at Cole is today an attractive private dwelling, the rubble from the demolition of Cole viaduct being used to back-fill the trackbed to bridge No 121.   *Both: R. C. Riley*

Above: BR Standard Class '5' No 73052 heads the 4.15pm stopping train from Evercreech Junction to Bournemouth West past Templecombe MPD on 7 July 1959. No 73052 was one of three members of the class, Nos 73050/1/2, allocated to the Somerset & Dorset when brand new in 1954. When delivered, No 73050 was absolutely immaculate having had a special exhibition finish to take part in the International Railway Congress Exhibition at Willesden. Class '2P' No 40634 (ex-SDJR No 45) can be seen on shed, its tablet catcher being clearly visible on the tender. This locomotive was withdrawn two years later as were all but one of the 4-4-0s which remained on the S&D. The tall building used as offices at Templecombe MPD was the former Dorset Central Railway station, the engine shed being rebuilt in 1950. *R.C. Riley*

Right: A fine portrait of BR Standard Class '5' No 73087 outside Templecombe MPD. Every year since 1956 No 73087 together with No 73116 was sent on loan to the S&D by Nine Elms (70A) MPD for the duration of the summer service. However, in 1960 No 73087 had arrived at Bath as usual, but not No 73116 which remained at Nine Elms although working through from Bournemouth occasionally. *R. C. Riley*

Left: Freshly outshopped from works, Class '4F' 0-6-0 No 44559 heads the 4.16pm from Evercreech Junction to Bournemouth West away from Templecombe on 12 July 1960. The pilot engine that has brought the train in from Templecombe SR can be seen in the distance at the signals close to Templecombe No 2 box. No 44559 was one of five standard MR Class '4Fs' built in 1922 by Armstrong Whitworth at their Newcastle works. Always known as 'Armstrongs' on the S&D where they were numbered 57-61. By pure chance when the LMS took over the S&DJR locomotive stock in 1930 the latest LMS Class '4F' was No 4556, the 'Armstrongs' remaining identifiable as 4557-61 with the prefix 4 being added at Nationalisation. *R.C. Riley*

Above: Bath (Green Park) MPD's BR Standard Class '4' No 75071 leaves Templecombe with the 3.20pm from Bath to Bournemouth West on 3 July 1961. With the S&D's increased allocation of these engines at this time, they worked most of the local services over the main line. All members of this class shedded at Templecombe having single chimneys. *R. C. Riley*

Above: Class '3F' 0-6-0 No 43248 (ex-S&DJR No 75) hauls the 3.40pm Bournemouth to Bristol up to the SR station on 7 July 1959, the train engine being BR Standard Class '4' No 75072. Note the 'Falling Man' type tablet catcher for northbound trains, the apparatus being in the safety position, the catcher jaws being seen on the left. Templecombe Junction signalbox was a 44-lever box of wooden construction and was the largest signal box on the line. On the single line to Broadstone just five chains beyond the box and the junction stood Templecombe Lower platform which was built on the up side of the single line in 1887. Because of its close proximity the shed, some trains which did not call at the SR station stopped there to enable a crew change to take place. By June 1962 only one surviving Class '3F' 0-6-0, No 43216, remained in traffic on the S&D. Built by Neilson, Reid & Co in 1902. Two months later she was also withdrawn from service. The SR station at Templecombe closed at the same time as the S&D but after 17 years reopened for Exeter to Salisbury passenger traffic in 1983.

R. C. Riley

Henstridge, the first station south of Templecombe on the S&D, was unusual in that it was the only station on the main line not to have a passing loop. The platform, at 150ft long, was also the shortest. It should be added that the 1928-built halt at Stourpaine & Durweston and the little used Templecombe Lower were also single line platforms. Photographed on 4 July 1961 it can be seen that there are two wagons in the siding which closed to goods traffic on 5 April 1965. Access to this siding was controlled by a small ground frame which was taken out of use on 6 July 1965.

R. C. Riley

Below: Stranger at Templecombe. Beattie 2-4-0WT No 30587 engages in shunting on 29 September 1962, presumably *en route* to the capital for railtour duties. As most S&D trains called at Templecombe Upper, this meant that they had either to be drawn in backwards by another engine if travelling in the up direction, or be drawn out in reverse if travelling down. Apart from those trains designed for push-pull working, it was a requirement that a passenger train had an engine at its leading end. This additional use of a second engine added to both time and expense, the extra locomotive being attached or detached at No 2 Junction. Had facilities been improved at Templecombe Lower economies could have been made.

J. Duncan Gomersall

Right: Maunsell Class 'S15' No 30824 powers a down fitted freight through Templecombe on 17 September 1962. One of 10 members of the class allocated to Salisbury (72B) MPD at that time, it was transferred to Feltham (70B) MPD in December 1963, where it became one of the last five members of the class to remain in traffic surviving until September 1965.

Alan Jarvis

Left: A fine panoramic view of Yeovil Town (83E) MPD taken in May 1964 in which a number of former GWR locomotives can be seen. These engines had been reallocated to Yeovil Town following the closure of the engine shed at Yeovil Pen Mill on 5 January 1959. The Beeching period brought many changes to Yeovil, the first being the withdrawal of the Taunton to Yeovil passenger service on 15 June 1964. However, the Yeovil Town to Pen Mill shuttle survived until 29 November 1965. After Yeovil Town closed on 2 October 1966, the Yeovil Town shuttle was transferred to Pen Mill via South Junction, but this only lasted until 6 May 1968. On the same day, Yeovil Town to Pen Mill, which had only been retained for access to the locomotive depot at Town, closed completely. Whilst Yeovil Pen Mill remains open today for passenger traffic, it closed to goods traffic on 3 January 1983. *Roy Hobbs*

Right: A detail study of Southern 'Unrebuilt' Light Pacific No 34067 *Tangmere* as it stands outside the depot at Yeovil Town on 18 May 1963. Even in its last years, Town shed continued to act as an overnight resting place for locomotives on their way from Devon and Cornwall to Eastleigh Works. When the veteran Beattie well tanks became due for overhaul at Eastleigh, local enthusiasts would know that these celebrated engines would stay overnight. *C. L. Caddy*

Above: The crew of 'M7' class 0-4-4T No 30129 pose for the camera at Yeovil Junction on 12 July 1962 as they prepare their loco for the trip to Town. In the late 1950s and early 1960s, the shuttle between the two Southern stations was normally in the care of one of the resident 0-4-4Ts No's 30129 and 30131 or 'O2' class No 30182. In the south of Somerset, the Southern Region was less impatient to convert to diesel traction, the practice of starting some trains at the Town instead of the Junction continued and a brace of Maunsell 'U' class 2-6-0s were usually allocated at Yeovil Town MPD for services originating locally, the last regular steam workings through the Yeovil area being the Westbury to Weymouth trains.

C. J. Gammell

Right: Another delightful study of 'M7' class 0-4-4T No 30129 at Yeovil Junction as it prepares to leave with the 6.33pm to the Town on 18 August 1962. Yeovil's lavish railway facilities were the result of fierce competition between the Great Western and London & South Western Railways.

J. Phillips/Courtesy: C. J. Gammell

A busy scene showing the rather cramped layout at the south end of Yeovil Pen Mill station on 13 June 1958 as 4-6-0 No 7015 *Carn Brea Castle* is prepared to depart with a train for Weymouth. Other locomotives in view are 'Prairie' 2-6-2T No 5522 and 0-6-0PT No 8745. On 8 August 1913 there was a tragic accident at Yeovil when an excursion train from Paddington to Weymouth was standing at the 'down' platform when a following express from Paddington hauled by No 3710 *City of Bath* ran into the back of it, two passengers being killed. The main line between Castle Cary and Dorchester Junction was singled in May and June 1968, the first stage, Castle Cary to Pen Mill, being carried out on 12 May when the layout at Yeovil Pen Mill was much simplified. The former 'down' main at Pen Mill was also signalled for two-way working at that stage. The sections from Castle Cary to Pen Mill and Maiden Newton were worked by electric token, although the section from Maiden Newton to Dorchester, which was singled on 9 June 1968, was worked by tokenless block.

Trevor B. Owen

Another view of the same train seen on the previous page as it heads for Weymouth past the diminutive shed at Pen Mill. The compact timber-built shed with a brick-built office was originally constructed as a broad gauge depot. Whilst it probably altered little in its lifetime, the coaling plant consisted of a coaling platform surmounted by a water tank with a timber lean-to providing wagon protection. Its allocation in 1947 was seven 0-6-0PTs, three 2-6-2Ts and six railcars.

Trevor B. Owen

Left: 0-6-0PT No 3787 carries out shunting duties at Chard Junction on 15 June 1962. When the end for steam locomotives came on BR it was closely followed by the rapid decline of the familiar operation of shunting. For more than a century the endless sorting of passenger coaches and wagons had been time consuming and labour intensive. The wasteful use of labour was reflected in the low wages paid to shunters and goods guards. Whilst shunting duties were often reserved for young men on the promotion ladder, the best jobs went to 'accommodated' drivers with eyesight and health problems. Shunters needed a good geographical knowledge of British railways if they were to carry out their duties efficiently.

R. C. Riley

Above: Decay and neglect have taken hold at Chard Central as 2-6-2T No 5504 is seen with a train from Chard Junction on 13 June 1958. By 1884 much of the GWR had been converted to the standard gauge, but east of Exeter, the only line on which the GWR retained the broad gauge was the Chard branch, conversion not taking place until July 1891.

Trevor B. Owen

0-6-0PT No 5798 has arrived at the Chard Central from Taunton on 13 June 1958. Whilst main line from Yeovil Junction to Exeter opened on 19 July 1860, it was not until 8 May 1863 that the 3½ mile branch to Chard, together with a canal tramway, was opened by the Chard Railway Co. This event meant that the station at Chard Road had to be renamed as Chard Junction, the title of the terminus being known as Chard Town. On 11 September 1866 the Bristol & Exeter Railway's broad gauge branch from Taunton was opened, and ran into Chard Joint station which was operated as a LSWR/B&E concern, the B&E having taken over the Chard Railway in 1864. The station at Chard Central, which had an overall roof, can be seen in this picture. This was the terminus of the Bristol & Exeter line, the standard gauge LSWR line running into the bay of the left hand side. The inscription 'Bristol & Exeter Booking Office' painted over the station doorway was still visible, even at closure, on 10 September 1962, the waiting room also having a South Devon Railway seat on this date.

Trevor B. Owen

A side view of the train shed at Chard Central as 0-6-0PT No 7436 prepares to depart on 13 June 1958. During World War 1 both the LSWR and the GWR had to make economies, the two companies entering negotiations to simplify operations at Chard. The outcome was that the LSWR abandoned passenger services into Chard Town, the GWR taking over the working of the line between Chard Joint and Chard Junction. By 1922 the GWR operated six trains each way between Taunton and Chard on weekdays with one extra from Taunton on Saturdays, journey time being around 40min. *R. C. Riley*

Left: 0-6-0PT No 9670 has arrived at Ilminster with a Taunton to Chard train on 14 June 1962. The 13-mile long line from Creech Junction, near Taunton, to Chard had been promoted by the Chard & Taunton Railway, stations being opened at Ilminster and Hatch. These were followed by the opening of a further station at Thorn in 1871. This remote station, some distance from the village it purported to serve, was renamed Thornfalcon in 1901. The station at Ilminster kept tickets for the unstaffed halts at Ilton and Donyatt. In 1901 the GWR's allocation of locomotives at Chard consisted of '517' class 0-4-2T No 544 and '1076' class 0-6-0ST No 1145. On 10 September 1962, passenger services were withdrawn between Taunton and Chard, not only on the WR section but also on the former SR section to Chard Junction.   *R. C. Riley*

Above: An unidentified 0-6-0PT waits at Hatch with a Chard to Taunton train in August 1962. The station at Hatch was an example of Bristol & Exeter broad gauge design with overhanging roof and ironwork roof brackets. By keeping the broad gauge the GWR felt that it would stop the LSWR obtaining running powers to Taunton, conversion to standard gauge being delayed until 1891   *J. Phillips/Courtesy C. J. Gammell*

Allocated to Taunton (83B) MPD some 12 months earlier, 2-6-2T No 4143 is seen at that station in August 1962. In August 1868 the Bristol & Exeter Co replaced the original station at Taunton, designed by Brunel. This new station was of more orthodox design and had an overall roof. In 1895 the GWR lengthened the platforms considerably and added bay platforms on both sides at each end. To the south of the station, a goods avoiding line was opened on 1 November 1896. Whilst modifications and extensions continued to be made for the next 34 years, a real rebuilding prgramme was not begun until September 1930. Over the next three years the overall roof was removed, the new West Junction and goods lines re-aligned and the track from Taunton East Junction to Creech Junction quadrupled. In addition to these works the two pairs of through platform lines were open between the East and West Junctions, the line thence to Norton Fitzwarren was quadrupled, whilst extensions and modifications continued right through the 1930s. As late as 1944 sidings were added to the West yard. In the 1896 rebuilding, a new engine shed was constructed and remained to service steam locomotives until 1964.

J. Phillips/ courtesy:C. J. Gammell

4-6-0 No 6954 *Lotherton Hall* waits to depart from Taunton with a down passenger train on 8 September 1962. Between 1962 and 1968 rationalisation of sidings at Taunton took place although these measures did not affect the layout at Taunton station. Despite these cut-backs in the 1960s the Coal Concentration scheme was adopted and was constructed near the East Junction signalbox, opening on 1 June 1964. The depot at Taunton was constructed with a northlight pattern roof, the period coal stage having the usual ramp approach with a corrugated lean-to for the coal wagons. In addition to the shed and coaling stage there were offices and standard repair shop, the latter being added in 1932. In the three years up to 1937 the cost of coal had increased by one third and Taunton was considered as the starting point for a proposed electrification programme which would have included all lines west of the town. The electrical consultants were Messrs Merz & McLellan, their report published in May 1939 concluded that the scheme would cost over £4,000,000 and was therefore abandoned. *C. L. Caddy*

Left: When the Bristol to Bath section of the GWR's line from Paddington to Bristol had been completed, the company was eager to promote its achievements. To this end a special train carried the directors and the Great Western's chief engineer, the diminutive Isambard Kingdom Brunel. This special made a trial run between the two cities, on 21 August 1840 and took 33min to cover the 11¾ miles, two stops being made *en route*. One of eight minutes at Keynsham station and another at Newton St Loe to pick up the company's resident civil engineer, George Frere. Ten days later the line was opened to the public, the first train consisting of five second-class carriages and three first-class vehicles, being hauled by a 2-2-2 locomotive *Fireball*. At that time Keynsham was the only intermediate stop, the stations at Saltford and Twerton not being opened until December 1840. Here, 2-8-2T No 7250 heads a PW rail train out of the western portal of Twerton tunnel on 30 July 1963.
C. G. Maggs

Right: A splendid action picture depicting 'King' class 4-6-0 No 6025 *King Henry III* as it leaves the eastern end of Whiteball tunnel with an up Paddington express on 9 June 1962. The fascination of Whiteball was the steep gradients in both directions which ensured relatively slow moving trains. The eastbound climb started gradually from Exeter with two miles of 1 in 155 then easing slightly before the last two miles to Whiteball at 1 in 115. The westbound climb was more severe and started gradually from Taunton getting steeper after Wellington with four miles at 1 in 90, 1 in 86, 1 in 80 and 1 in 127, the summit being reached near Whiteball Siding. Depending on the class of locomotive being used, the heavier trains in this direction would stop at Wellington for a Taunton '51xx' class banker to come on at the rear, no bankers being required for the eastbound climb. *Peter W. Gray*

Left: '43xx' Class 2-6-0 No 7337 ambles into Wiveliscombe with a Taunton to Barnstaple train on 14 September 1963. At that time residents in the area discovered a way to avoid paying the full price for a season ticket. They would purchase runabout circular tour tickets at £1 per head and commute the 40 odd miles into Barnstaple — a much cheaper option. The Taunton to Barnstaple line still had quite a few relics even in 1963. There were Bristol & Exeter Railway chairs in the waiting room at South Molton and B&ER luggage labels still in the racks at Morebath and South Molton having been there 89 years since the railway opened. The railway opened as far as Wiveliscombe on 8 June 1871, finally reaching Barnstaple on 1 November 1873, criss-crossing the border of Somerset and Devon. *Alan Jarvis*

Above: Another 'Mogul' 2-6-0, No 7333, enters Venn Cross with a Barnstaple to Taunton train on 14 September 1963. Whilst this station was strictly in Devon, the county boundary came very close to the platform end. Passenger services between Taunton and Barnstaple were withdrawn on 3 October 1966 although the line had lost its freight facilities in 1964. *Alan Jarvis*

Above: A splendid picture showing what delights railway stations offered the traveller over 30 years ago. This view was taken at Dulverton station on 22 August 1959. Whilst the Devon & Somerset Railway opened its line to Barnstaple on 1 November 1873, it was not until 1 August 1884 that the Exe Valley branch from Tiverton joined the Barnstaple line at Morebath Junction Halt.

Right: Also seen on 22 August 1959, 0-6-0PT No 9765 waits to depart from Dulverton with an Exe Valley train. The Devon & Somerset Railway, which became the GWR's Barnstaple branch, was worked by the Bristol & Exeter from the outset and although it remained nominally independent until 1901. It had not been successful, arrears in interest payments to share-holders amounting to over £500,000.

Designed by Collett the '57XX' class of pannier tanks totalled 843 and represented the largest single class of locomotives operated by British Railways. By the time that No 9765 was photographed, the first members of the class had been withdrawn. It was to be a further eight years before the last of the class disappeared, No 9765 being withdrawn from Exeter St Davids (83C) MPD in December 1961.   *Both: Alan Jarvis*

'Prairie' 2-6-2T No 4143 is being prepared to depart from Minehead with a train for Taunton and Paddington in August 1963. One of the longest lines to operate today the West Somerset Railway is one of preservation's success stories. Opened as a broad gauge line in July 1874, the West Somerset Railway was the last line to be engineered under the auspices of Brunel. Operated by the Bristol & Exeter Railway, the first section from Taunton to Watchet opened on 31 March 1864. Whilst passenger services on the Taunton to Barnstaple line were withdrawn from 3 October 1966, those on the Minehead branch continued until 2 January 1971. The station at Minehead, which had been greatly extended by the GWR in 1934, was reopened little more than five years after closure. *R. E. Toop*

Former Cardiff Railway 0-4-0ST No 1338 is seen at Bridgwater docks on 7 July 1959. Nominally allocated to Taunton MPD in 1943, No 1338 was in fact based at the sub-shed at Bridgwater for dock shunting. At that time commercial shipping at Bridgwater had been in decline for some years, the services of No 1338 finally being considered unnecessary in June 1960 when it joined a string of other different 0-4-0STs to shunt at Swansea docks. By February 1955 No 1338 had become the last ex-Cardiff Railway locomotive to operate on British Railways and continued in service until September 1963. Speed over the docks branch was limited to 5mph as the line crossed six public roads, the engines only being allowed to operate in daylight and clear weather. Stop signals were provided on either side of the opening bridge, stop blocks having to be placed across the rails. The line to a wharf on the River Parrett had previously been a horse tramway before acquisition by the Bristol & Exeter Railway in 1863 and was converted to a mixed gauge locomotive line in 1867. Following closure of the Somerset & Dorset Bridgwater North branch, a connection was provided from the Docks branch to Bridgwater North station in 1954, the docks branch closing in 1967.

R.C. Riley

The station nameboard is still intact in this picture of the closed station at Sandford & Banwell on 21 June 1965. The 31¾ mile branch from Yatton to Witham had closed to passengers on 7 September 1963, the last train being hauled by 0-6-0 No 3218 of Wells shed. In its later years the passenger services were generally worked by BR Standard 2-6-2Ts, the ex-GWR 0-6-0s tending to be kept for freight duties. As trains were restricted to 12 loaded coal wagons up the grade from Wells and Shepton Mallet, they were often split into two parts up the 1 in 37 bank at Wanstrow. The section between Yatton and Cheddar was opened on 3 August 1869 and had intermediate stations at Congresbury, Sandford, Woodborough and Axbridge, Woodborough being renamed Winscombe on 30 October 1869. Until September 1985 the section between Cranmore and Witham continued to see use for bitumen traffic to the tanker yard adjacent to Cranmore station.   *R. C. Riley*

Looking east at Yatton station on 22 August 1962, Ivatt Class '2MT' 2-6-2T No 41245 is being prepared to depart with the 2.45pm to Witham. When the section of the branch between Cheddar and Wells opened there were intermediate stations at Lodge Hill and Draycott, the line becoming popular with strawberry pickers in the summer months, it was known as the 'Strawberry Line'. As a result of rationalisation by the Great Western in 1877 the East Somerset Railway station at Wells was closed, passenger traffic being concentrated at Tucker Street. After its closure to passengers, the original East Somerset Railway station became the GWR's goods depot. *C. G. Maggs*

Above: As the Western Region of BR increased its influence on the former S&D lines the ex-GWR Collett 0-6-0s were drafted in to replace the Class '3F' 0-6-0s, the last of which was withdrawn in 1962. Here, an unidentified Collett 0-6-0 heads a short train on the Highbridge to Evercreech Junction branch near Bason Bridge in October 1964. The principal activity at Bason Bridge was the milk factory owned by United Dairies which loaded rail milk tanks for London. After the Burnham-on-Sea and Highbridge Wharf lines had been closed on 16 May 1965, the crossing at Highbridge was altered to enable the continuation of milk traffic from Bason Bridge creamery, a direct connection being made from the S&D line to the ex-GWR goods yard on the west side of the up line. This enabled the section from Bason Bridge to Highbridge to remain in use until 2 October 1972, some years after the closure of the rest of the branch. *Alan Jarvis*

Right: Class '3F' 0-6-0 No 43248 (ex-S&DJR No 75) passes the box at Highbridge East as it heads the 2.20pm to Evercreech Junction on 7 July 1959. With the Burnham-on-Sea branch losing its passenger traffic in 1951 and freight traffic in 1963, Highbridge became the latter day terminus of the branch. Most of the S&D locomotive works buildings at Highbridge closed in 1930, although many remained derelict but intact when the line closed in 1966. *R. C. Riley*

Left: Ivatt Class '2' 2-6-2Ts Nos 41307 & 41283 head the LCGB's 'Mendip Merchantman' railtour away from Glastonbury towards Highbridge on 1 January 1966. This tour was drafted before it was known that the Western Region's planned closure of the S&D for 3 January 1966 had been postponed. Not withstanding this the railtour went ahead as planned, the train being hauled into Templecombe behind SR 'Merchant Navy' No 35011 *General Steam Navigation.*

Above: Also on 1 January 1966, Ivatt Class '2' 2-6-2 No 41290 stands in the station at Glastonbury with the 1.15pm from Evercreech Junction against the backdrop of the well-known landmark of Glastonbury Tor. This station was situated on the Evercreech Junction to Burnham-on-Sea branch of the S&DJR system. Regular passenger services to Burnham were cut back to Highbridge (East) on 29 October 1951, although the nominally closed section continued to be used for excursion traffic until 8 September 1962, occasional freight working continuing until 20 May 1963. One reason which probably predisposed this closure was the fact that the line immediately west of Highbridge (S&D) crossed the GWR main line between Bristol and Taunton by means of a level crossing. No doubt the cost of operating and maintaining this facility was taken into account before total shutdown was effected.

Both:Roy Hobbs

Above: 0-6-0PT No 4655 is seen passing the signalbox at Athelney on 12 July 1962. When the Yeovil branch opened, Athelney was one of three intermediate stations, the others being Langport and Martock. In pre-Grouping years, seven trains each way were timetabled, none taking less than one hour for the 20-mile journey.

C. J. Gammell

Right: Yeovil-based Class '4575' No 4593 passes the shelter on the staggered up platform at Martock with a Taunton to Yeovil Pen Mill train on 30 May 1964. One early casualty of Dr Beeching's 'surgery', the line closed to passengers on 15 June 1964 and with the opening of the Freight Concentration Depot at Taunton, goods traffic ceased on 6 July 1964, after which the line closed com-pletely. Just before closure the track layout at Martock was rationalised, the shunt neck spur being removed at the same time as the trailing connection 'down' main to the crane road and the trailing connection 'up' main to the goods shed. These removals taking place on 20 December 1963. At the same time signals 3 and 24 were recovered.

Trevor B. Owen

Below: Only three months before withdrawal, 'Prairie' 2-6-2T No 4569 shunts an engineer's train at Castle Cary in April 1964. Situated on the Great Western's 'new direct route to the West', Castle Cary provided a convenient jumping off point for the remainder of the route through Somerton and Langport (East), joining the old main line at Cogload.   *John Wiltshire*

Right: 0-6-0PT No 9615 has arrived at Frome with a train from Bristol via Radstock on 22 August 1959. Following Nationalisation in 1948 the number of weekday trains on the Frome branch was eight in each direction, but by the late 1950s passenger receipts had dwindled and a reduction of the services in 1958 failed to return the line into profit. This lead to an inevitable

closure, passenger services being withdrawn from 31 October 1959. On this day the last train left Frome for Bristol behind Ivatt Class '2MT' 2-6-2T No 41203. The five carriages were so heavily loaded that banking assistance was given by 0-6-0PT No. 9612 as far as Mells Road. However, the line remained open for freight until 1967.   *Alan Jarvis*

Left: A sylvan scene at New Frome Quarry in October 1964 as Sentinel No 3 (Works No 9387 of 1948) is assisted with a rake of trucks by an unidentified 0-6-0PT. This company has worked a number of quarries to the northwest of Frome and was formerly known as Roads Reconstruction (1934) Ltd. These were served by a 2ft 0in gauge tramway which was superseded by a standard gauge line in 1943, the 2ft 0in gauge lines being lifted in 1945. This 4ft 8½in gauge line was some two miles long and connected Whatley Quarry with the former GWR line from Frome to Radstock near Hapsford. This line passed through a short tunnel which was later replaced about 1966 by a larger new bore alongside. This in turn was also replaced by an entirely new shorter link from Whatley Quarry to new exchange sidings with BR. This includes two long tunnels and a viaduct which passes over the old alignment, the old line from the junction west of Great Elm level crossing via Hapsford was then lifted around November 1974.

Above: 1929-built Peckett (Works No 1788) is seen shunting at Kilmersdon Colliery in September 1971. The colliery was connected to the Radstock to Frome branch by a standard gauge line of which part was a rope worked incline. Locomotives worked between the colliery and the head of the incline. In addition to this work, engines also worked a line serving dirt tips to the west of the colliery, this being handled by road haulage after 1940. The colliery closed in October 1973.

Both: Alan Jarvis

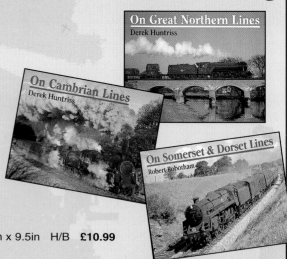